GOD Had Other *Plans*

VOLUME 1

TAMEKA HOPE

God Had Other Plans, Vol. I
Copyright © 2015 Tameka Hope

All rights reserved. No part of this book may be reproduced, distributed or transmitted in any form by any means, graphics, electronics, or mechanical, including photocopy, recording, taping, or by any information storage or retrieval system, without permission in writing from the publisher, except in the case of reprints in the context of reviews, quotes, or references.

Unless otherwise indicated, scripture quotations are from the Holy Bible, *New International Version®*, NIV® Copyright© 1973, 1978, 1984, 2011 by Biblica, Inc.®. All rights reserved.

Published by: Purposely Created Publishing Group™
Printed in the United States of America

ISBN-10: 1-942-83811-5
ISBN-13: 978-1-942838-11-1

Special discounts are available on bulk quantity purchases by book clubs, associations and special interest groups. For details email: sales@publishyourgift.com
or call (866) 674-3340.

For more information, log onto
www.PublishYourGift.com

Dedication

In loving memory of my two grandmothers,
Elizabeth Sudduth and Georgia Eatmon,
and my uncle, Alvernis Sudduth.

Look! I did it, and I will not stop here!

You're not here to see me prosper, but I know you are looking down on me and smiling.

I love you always.

Table of Contents

Acknowledgments		vii
The Lord is My Refuge: Psalm 91		ix
Chapter 1	*My Loving Family*	1
Chapter 2	*Raging Storms*	7
Chapter 3	*It Lasted How Long?*	11
Chapter 4	*Amidst the Confusion*	17
Chapter 5	*The Calm*	21
Chapter 6	*Cleaning Our Lives*	25
Chapter 7	*More Troubles*	33
Chapter 8	*A Little Bit of Happiness*	37
Chapter 9	*Another Loss*	41
Chapter 10	*A Fresh Start*	51
Chapter 11	*God's Angel*	55
Chapter 12	*God Has Other Plans*	59
About the Author		65

Acknowledgments

I give all glory, honor and praise to God. I thank God for His grace, mercy, and His angels! I would like to give thanks to my pastor, first lady, and church family. I give thanks also to one other local pastor and family in Downtown Tuscaloosa, Alabama.

I am blessed and grateful for my husband, Anthony and three children, Ta'mya, Zahria, and Anthony, Jr. You four have supported me through good and bad. To my husband, I thank you for being patient, loving, acceptable and willing to care of me and be by my side no matter what each day brought me with my health. It's a blessing to have you as a best friend/husband, and I love you dearly with all my heart!

To my two daughters, you young ladies rock! You are my *everything*. Continue to grow up, loving and treating others with the utmost respect. Remember to keep God first in your lives. I also want to thank my son, one of the most important men in my life, for staring me in the eyes. Each time I held and fed you, you gave me life and strength to keep pressing on my way.

God Had Other Plans

I give thanks to my mom and dad, Mrs. and Mr. Burton, who are always and forever there to pick up any loose ends. I love you both with all my heart! Last, but not least, I give thanks to a host of family, friends and many more. I can't forget the mayor of our city, as well as governmental and presidential authorities for going above and beyond to assist us through all that we endured.

I would also like to thank each and every one of my supporters, readers and followers. I hope my testimony leads you all closer to God. I hope it encourages you to go a step further in being obedient to do what God tells you to do. Chase your dreams, achieve your goals, and be all that your heart desires you to be. There is a BLESSING in the PRESSING. Without God, we are nothing. I leave you with the best part of my name, **HOPE**!

I love you all and pray that God will take care of all your needs with the wonderful blessings that come from Christ Jesus! (Philippians 4:19)

PSALM 91

Whoever dwells in the shelter of the Most High
    will rest in the shadow of the Almighty.[a]
I will say of the LORD, "He is my refuge and my fortress,
    my God, in whom I trust."
Surely he will save you
    from the fowler's snare
    and from the deadly pestilence.
He will cover you with his feathers,
    and under his wings you will find refuge;
    his faithfulness will be your shield and rampart.
You will not fear the terror of night,
    nor the arrow that flies by day,
    nor the pestilence that stalks in the darkness,
    nor the plague that destroys at midday.

God Had Other Plans

A thousand may fall at your side,
>ten thousand at your right hand,
>but it will not come near you.

You will only observe with your eyes
>and see the punishment of the wicked.

If you say, "The LORD is my refuge,"
>and you make the Most High your dwelling,

no harm will overtake you,
>no disaster will come near your tent.

For he will command his angels concerning you
>to guard you in all your ways;

they will lift you up in their hands,
>so that you will not strike your foot against a stone.

You will tread on the lion and the cobra;
>you will trample the great lion and the serpent.

"Because he[b] loves me," says the LORD, "I will rescue him;
>I will protect him, for he acknowledges my name.

He will call on me, and I will answer him;
>I will be with him in trouble,
>I will deliver him and honor him.

With long life I will satisfy him
>and show him my salvation."

Chapter 1

My Loving Family

I'm a mother of three: two girls and one boy. When I began this book, I was dating Anthony Hope, the father of my two youngest children. Because he's such a loving and honorable man, he is also raising my first born daughter as his own.

Anthony, also known as Nard or Ant, and I grew up together seeing as though our mothers are best friends and have been before we were born. Our families are so close that we called each other cousins when we were little. On top of that, we only lived about five minutes from one another. It's one of those small town stories because he actually babysat for his sister and me when we were small. We did everything together. When his family had a special occasion, we were there, and it was the same when our family had a special occasion.

Though we were like family, we weren't. We shared our first kiss over a game of truth or dare and bought each other things as bribes for keeping secrets, but for the longest time, we'd never dated. One day, his mom caught us kissing. She was coming out of the bathroom and walked right in on us while our lips were glued together. My mom had this thing she did whenever she spanked me and my sister called the right shoe. I must say I gave him that kiss, but I paid for it with a spanking.

As we grew older, I began to go on dates. Nard also dated and started hanging out late. He even found new friends outside of his neighborhood. Adrian, Nard's younger sister, and I started doing our girl thing while Nard and his little brother, Thomas, did theirs. They'd leave early in the morning and not come back until late at night.

Soon, Nard started getting into a lot of trouble, which landed him in detention centers. He eventually went to jail, and then he went to prison for seven years. While in prison, he began working and became a productive member of society. As he struggled to find his place in life, I graduated high school and started college.

Free, young, and living my life in college, I was doing pretty good for a 20-year-old young lady. I didn't have any kids and I made my own money, so I did a good bit of travelling. Living life to the fullest, me and my best friend, Angela, along with a few other very close friends, would party every single night. When Angela began dating Mon, we slowed our partying all the way down. I started working a lot and hanging with my cousin, Brenda, and some other friends. I'd also spend time with a guy named Mario who I'd been friends with since sixth grade. Romantically, it really wasn't serious, but he did father my oldest daughter, Ta'mya.

I slowed down a whole lot after giving birth to my daughter because I always said that I didn't want any kids until I was married or in a relationship with the father. When I had my daughter, her father and I got along well for a while. As months and years passed, I often shared with my mom and Diamond, Nard's mom, that I wanted a good man. One night, Diamond said, "Well Mek, why don't you wait for my son? I think y'all would be good for each other. I know it's been years, but he's a good man, and he just needs a good woman."

I had not seen or spoken to Nard in almost ten years because I was always on the go. Whenever he called, Diamond and Adrian were either at their house or I'd be at my house. I heard Diamond, but I didn't count on it or think about it anymore after that night. A year passed, and it was November 2006, time for Nard to come home. He came over to my mom's house the day he got out, but I'd already left for work. I saw him about four days later when I visited Adrian. When I parked the car in front of the house, he was standing outside. I got out of my car and hugged him. I must admit, his body was nice. As we spent time catching up, both of us were blushing. He was staying at Adrian's house, but his momma was talking to my mom, and it was somehow discussed that he wanted to chill for a minute.

I told my mom and Diamond that he could stay at my apartment. I was only there on the weekend because my baby was always at my mom's house while I worked at night. Before I knew it, Nard started spending nights at my apartment. I gave him his space, and I had mine. Each day, from the first day he was there, he wanted to do things together. If I left before he woke up, he would call and ask if he could just spend time with me. It didn't matter if I was just shopping or getting a manicure, he just wanted to be with me.

One morning, for instance, he came in my daughter's room and asked if I'd let him take me out to eat and to the movies. I said yes, and as time passed, we became serious. He was definitely a man I could see myself settling down with. He told me he had never been in a serious relationship and never had a girlfriend that he was serious about. Nonetheless, he and I discussed becoming a couple, but he said he wanted to talk to the family about it first. I didn't tell him that his mom told me to wait for him until we found that I was pregnant with his first child. Needless to say, our families were happy that we had become a couple.

Chapter 2

Raging Storms

As a family, we had been experiencing a setback. I had just returned back to work at Piggly Wiggly, a local grocery store, after giving birth to my son, Junior. I worked full-time until I found out that I was pregnant with my third child and began to have morning sickness. Though it was called morning sickness, I was actually sick all day, so I cut my hours down to part-time. Nard's hours were reduced around the same time, so the household was financially tight.

My job, money, and bills were a constant worry. I remember fussing and cursing about a bill. I said, "I'm sick of living check to check. Shit can't get any worse." Anthony was standing in the living room. He turned to face me and said, "We are blessed. There are people in this country starving and waiting for the things we have, so don't ever say it can't get worse because it can. This is nothing that we're experiencing."

God Had Other Plans

Not long after that, a tornado touched down in Tuscaloosa, Alabama. It damaged a whole neighborhood on Loop Road. A tree fell on the rear end of our house, but thank God, there was no damage. Nard and I, along with our landlords, Mr. and Mrs. Caddy, got together to pick up the pieces of the tree. The following Saturday, we were on our way to my mother's house when we saw the Red Cross riding through the neighborhood. The driver stopped and asked if we wanted bottles of water or food. Anthony turned it down, then we saw people sitting on their front porch and in their yards picking up their belongings. I cried and explained to our kids what happened. I also told them how important it was to help people in need.

Each day from this point, we watched the weather channel. Tornados were damaging homes in other states daily. People were losing their family members, their homes, their cars, and their lives. I became frightened and was very afraid to sleep in the two rooms in the back of the house whenever it rained or during threats of bad weather. I'd pray for the people who had lost their things and family in the storms, and I didn't say it out loud, but I was wondering how people could say, "I can't find my car or spouse." I also found myself always wanting to gather the kids to keep them safe, wanting them to sleep in the front rooms because there wasn't a tree over that part of the house.

Tuesday evening, on April 26th, 2011, it was pouring down raining. Tuscaloosa News issued a severe weather warning for Tuscaloosa and the surrounding counties until Wednesday morning. I told everyone that we should all sleep in the front room because I was worried about that tree falling on the house. Nard said, "Tameka, let's get down and say our family prayer. We're all sleeping in the rooms as normal because you can't run. When it's your time, it's gone get you." So we did just that.

The next morning, April 27th, we were at home in our house on 10th Avenue, across the street from Rosedale Court apartments. Around 5 AM, my mom called and said the news had reported a tornado on the ground in Northport, Alabama. Northport and Tuscaloosa are separated on one side by the Black Warrior River, which was about ten minutes away from our home. Anthony flipped on the television, then Momma started screaming, "They said to get in a safe place."

Anthony ran to get the kids, and we all headed for the hall. We could hear the rain and wind outside. Anthony gets us all in the hall then realizes that he'd parked around the back of the house underneath that tree, so he ran out and pulled his truck to the side before rushing back in. We were packed in this small unsafe hall with doorway openings and windows in all directions, but the kids were still covered safely. The sirens were going off, the wind was pushing against the window screens, and I was praying to God for Him to protect and shield us. We all sat together, listening for the rain and sirens to stop. It lasted for about ten minutes, then we didn't hear anything but the wind and thunder. It was about 6:20 when the storm stopped. Anthony said, "Nobody is going to school or work today. Let's all go back to bed." I called and told my boss that I would be late. I heard Anthony clearly, but I still decided to go to work. I really didn't want to go, but I had already missed some days when I was sick, so I set my alarm to 8 AM.

Chapter 3

It Lasted How Long?

It was sunny outside, and the birds were singing. It was a beautiful spring day. I got dressed and let Nard take me to work. On the way there, he said, "Tameka, if it's storming when you get off, I'm not gon' bring the kids out in it." I agreed and told him that I would be okay. I could always climb in a cooler until it was over.

When I arrived to work, I was the only cashier there. Everybody else said they couldn't make it because of down power lines or trees blocking the road. I started questioning why I was at work instead of with my family. The general manager even said he needed to leave because a tree fell on his house. Hours passed, and I started feeling worried. I felt that something was going to happen, and I needed to be with my family. I told a co-worker about my feelings and then told the assistant manager that I wanted to leave. He laughed and said that if I could find someone to come in to take my place, I could leave. I called everybody, but nobody would come in to work. All that day, I kept feeling like I should be with my family.

In the front of the store, there were only glass windows. As a cashier, I was right up front, so we kept an eye on the weather. Every customer who walked in talked about the tornado that hit earlier that morning. They were also saying that another tornado was coming around three or four that afternoon. My manager kept updating me with the weather, so I texted and called Nard to check on him and the kids. The store wasn't that crowded, and everybody was saying they were trying to get home before the storm came.

As 3 PM approached, the sky became cloudy. The wind increased and customers came in spreading weather updates. I went to the back of the store to call Anthony. I wondered if he was on the way because earlier he told me if it was storming when I got off, he wasn't going to bring the kids out. When he answered, he said they were on their way. The clock struck 2:30 and I took my last 15 minute break and grabbed up a few dry and canned foods so we would have something in case the power went out.

By the time I got off at three, the wind was blowing harder and the sky was getting darker. I called Nard, and he said they were about to turn into the parking lot. On our way home, we listened to the news. They were following and reporting all the other towns and states that were hit by tornados. The newscast gave a 3:35 PM warning for the second tornado and said it was traveling in different towns headed for Tuscaloosa. Nard asked if I wanted to stay at home or go over my mother's house. I told him to go home and wait for another weather update.

When we pulled into the yard, a red, black and blue colored bird dropped down on the fence next to the truck where we were sitting. The bird looked at the tree that fell in the back of the house weeks before during another storm and looked back at us. It's like the bird was warning us not to stay. We went in the house, and Nard checked the news. I sat my purse and a few bags on the counter, and then the sirens sounded. The newscaster advised everyone to find a safe place for the next hour, so we decided to go to my mother's house, which was about 20 minutes away from our house.

I remember seeing kids playing and people sitting outside like there was no siren or warning given. Once at my mother's house, our three kids, Anthony, my mom, my dad, and my two sisters sat together watching the local news. It was about 4:45 PM when the power shut off, and the last thing I remember was Jamie Spain, the local meteorologist, saying there was a tornado spotted on Skyland Boulevard near McFarland Mall. Since the power shut off, Anthony stepped out on the back porch to look over the house. The door shut behind him and locked.

He looked up and saw the tornado heading towards the house. He began beating on the patio door. My daddy opened the door, and Anthony was yelling, "Get in the bathtub!" We all ran into the bathroom. My mom and dad went in the bathroom inside their bedroom while, Anthony, me, our three kids, and my two sisters, Erin and Tanika, went in the bathroom in the center of the hallway. It sounded like a train and shook the house like an earthquake. I prayed until I heard the noise go away. Though it was more like seven or eight minutes, it felt like it lasted about twenty minutes.

When the noise stopped, my daddy came out of the second bathroom and called out to make sure we all were okay. He and Anthony headed out the front door. I started to follow, but I heard someone say that it was coming back. Then I saw the debris blow inside as the door rushed back against the wall. I ran back into the bathtub until Anthony came in and said everything was over.

The tornado hit around 5:10 PM. It did more damage than any other tornado in Alabama history. The National Weather Service determined the path length of this violent tornado to be 80.3 miles with a maximum damage path width of 1.5 miles. The preliminary classification was an EF-4 tornado with winds up to 190 mph. However, they later upgraded it to an EF-5.

Chapter 4

Amidst the Confusion

As I walked into the front yard, I noticed Anthony's truck window was gone, and my mom's house had some roof and siding damage. Nard's co-worker was out of town in Mississippi, so Anthony called to check on them. He asked us to go by and check on their house, so we did that first. They lived on Skyland Boulevard which was about ten minutes away from my mother's house. On our way there, we saw a few trees damaged because of wind, but his co-worker didn't have much damage near his house.

We drove to check on our home when Mel, Anthony's brother, called and told Anthony that the apartments in front of our house were destroyed by the tornado. The phone lines were crossed, but somehow Anthony still received the call. Mel said, "Man, the whole Rosedale Court is gone."

It took us about 30 minutes to make it to our side of town. Traffic was heavy and trees were down everywhere, so we had to take a detour to get to the house. The traffic was so backed up because everybody in Tuscaloosa was trying to get over to the area where we lived, wanting to see the damage and check on their loved ones. Because the emergency responders were blocking the streets, we had to park at Chevron and walk about five minutes to our house.

"Listen, if you don't want to do this, we can turn around. I can tell you now that tree is gone, and I'm sure the house is too," Anthony said. I decided to continue, and as we were walking, I saw my cousin Lashawn's car. I called out for her and she ran up and hugged me long and tight. She said, "Thank you, Jesus, you all are okay!" She said that her boyfriend Tommy had walked ahead to see if he could find us. We began to walk towards the house, and Tommy walked up to us, looking as if he saw a ghost. When he saw us, he began to hug me and Anthony.

We kept walking up 10th Avenue to my house and people were lodged under debris, reaching for our legs, screaming for help and oxygen. The emergency responders placed the oxygen tanks on them and strapped them to stretchers. We were also stepping over dead bodies. I was in total shock and sick to my stomach. I cried, remembering seeing people dead with cars and other things on top of them. It was unbelievable, like a movie or news footage of New Orleans. I looked to my right and noticed there were no homes on the row that we lived.

Before the storm, there were six or seven homes on our row. Anthony and I kept walking back and forth as if this was a dream, but it was real. Not one house was still standing. One of our kid's toys and a photobook I made years ago was at my feet, and only the foundation of what we once had was in that spot that was our home. I stood there and just looked at the things that we had called our own.

My neighbor began to rise from the debris which covered her for safety. She was carrying a mop bucket with a pair of house slippers and was still wearing her sleeping clothes. Around this time of day, she always rested before going to work at night. While Anthony and I were checking on the house, it began to rain and get dark. People started to run, saying another tornado was on its way, so we ran back to the car and headed back to my mom's house.

On the way back, we drove along Greensboro Avenue and crossed over McFarland Boulevard to get on 37th Street by Bowers Park. We took Loop Road until we crossed over to Crescent Ridge Road. We had to park and walk about eight miles to my mother's neighborhood because the National Guard blocked the road due to the amount of deaths and severe damage done on Crescent Ridge and Holt Road. There were people walking with clothes, bags and babies, trying to make it to a church so they could have somewhere to sleep. It was so depressing.

On the way back, I was wondering how in the hell we were going to tell the kids they didn't have a room or a home. Carrying a headache and an upset stomach, my mind and nerves were on edge. I couldn't hear anything. All that played in my brain was the foundation where my house once stood.

Chapter 5

The Calm

Everything at this point seemed like a movie. When we made it back to my mom's side of town, the National Guard blocked off the road, so everybody who lived on Crescent Ridge Road or Holt had to walk in and out. After all, it was reported that the most fatalities were in Holt on Crescent Ridge Road. All that night, after the tornado passed through Tuscaloosa, everything was so peaceful. It was like God had come and calmed everything. The world had stopped and started back over, but everybody was helping each other this time. It wasn't one person who was unwilling to help the next.

After returning to my mother's house, we took showers and went to bed. Neither one of us was in our right mind. I couldn't sleep because it felt like my insides had been ripped out of me, and the tears wouldn't stop. We just lay there, on our backs, looking at the ceiling. As daybreak approached, I really found my nerves taking over me because I knew the kids' questions had to be answered.

Knock, knock. "Momma, it's me, Mya. Grandma Faye Faye said Ivina wants to speak to you." Ivina is one of my close friends, just like a sister. She wanted to make sure we were okay and to let me know she and her family were going to get with us that afternoon to donate.

My phone went dead the night of the tornado after trying to talk to my other close friend, Angela, as we both battled the traffic to get to our destinations before the second storm. The power was off throughout the entire Holt area. I had to let my phone charge in the truck. When it finally charged, I logged into my Facebook account and saw a message and a friend request from a young lady named Kris.

The message read: "Hello, Tameka. I hope all is well with you and your family. I have your social security information. It fell out of the air in front of my home. I am praying and hoping you all are okay and safe." I replied back: "Thank you, we are all alive, but we lost our home. Can we please stay in contact with each other?"

Tears were all over my hand and shirt. Things were just crazy and unbelievable. Friday morning, we gathered our three kids and climbed in the car to pick up my check from my job and find some canned milk for our five-month-old son. When we got to the end of the road where the National Guards were standing, they said nobody could leave or come in at that point. I tried explaining where we were going when the announcement came over the radio station that President Obama was in town and was headed in that direction. When they said he was in town, I knew it was very serious then. I didn't know how to feel about it though because I was in another state of mind, thinking of finding a place to get my son some milk.

We were confused, and I got upset because I had to feed my child. The guard explained if we went out, we couldn't return because there was a gas leak and everybody had to evacuate the Alberta City and Holt area. We took the kids to see our place, which, again, was nothing but the foundation. When they walked up to the street, they were quiet and just looking stunned. A few Fox 6 news reporters were standing around looking at everybody viewing the damage. I stepped into what was once our living room and began looking through things worth saving. I found a Bible, some school applications for my baby girl's preschool entry, and some old pictures. There was a very foul smell under the couch that was now turned over in kitchen, but I didn't bother to see what it was. I figured it was the kitten that would go under the house. I looked up and saw the news man filming me, and I immediately got upset because I wanted some privacy as I went through our things. At this point, I was headed straight for the camera man. Anthony noticed the man and the look on my face. I also saw in his eyes that he had gotten a little overwhelmed as well. He called out for us to leave, which we did because it was a bit much to take in. We headed back to the car and started on our way. I met up with the guy from FEMA, showed him our spot, gave him some information, and left.

Chapter 6

Cleaning Our Lives

We were riding everyday, looking for a place to call home. Anthony thought about his autographed Kobe Bryant jersey that held such great value. He was saving the jersey to give to our son when he grew up, but decided that it was best to go look for it. He found it in the back by the fence and also called to tell me that the odor we smelled was the body of a child buried underneath our old couch. I instantly went into deep thought about how that could have been one of our kids. It made me realize that I should be thankful we didn't decide to stay at our own house that day. I think it kind of touched Anthony when he found out it was a little boy.

My friends are very loving and willing ladies, so we do our best to be part of one another's life. Some of them came by my mother-in-law's house to drop off some clothes for the kids and some toiletries for me and Anthony. It's always good to give a helping hand to others because you never know when you will be in need.

My sister-in-law and I were at my mother-in-law's house cooking and having a few drinks. Following the storm, I turned to alcohol to help me deal with the depression of losing my home and everything in it. I had at least four drinks a day. Liquor, beer, wine, or mixed...You name it; I drunk it. I found myself drinking as soon as I woke up, sometimes before eating food. One morning, I even thought about buying a sack of weed and just sitting in the back yard getting high and crying my heart out.

Time was ticking. Although, my mother-in-law wasn't rushing us, it was well overdue. We stayed with Anthony mom's for about two and a half weeks before I found a house in a subdivision in West Tuscaloosa. I knew this was nothing but God because it had no sign on it, and the yard was exactly what I had asked God for. I went to the house on the end where some guys were sitting in the yard and asked for information. They led me directly to the owner. After six questions and a prayer, it was mine.

The landlord was very humble and a blessing to my family and me. I had to fix a few things, but after telling Mr. Thomas our situation, he completely understood and fixed everything within a day or two. My family was also adopted by a Baptist church. They took us and a few other families in for a few months. They even did an outpouring of blessings to us.

Although the tornado was a disaster, it turned out to be a blessing in so many ways. I had not worked in months and Anthony's job had a layoff. God made sure the children didn't lack anything and blessed us so that all the bills were paid. During the recovery of getting our lives back together, the loss of our home really weighed heavily on Anthony's heart. After going through the tornado and God sparing our lives, Anthony said, "Okay, Tameka. We gon' do this the right way. No more shacking."

Not only was that day a wake-up call for him, but for me as well. I decided that I wanted to go back to school, so I started applying for financial aid. I wasn't able to start that following semester, so I decided to go back to work as I waited. My very first day back at work, my heart began beating very fast after watching Anthony pull off. I walked in and felt lightheaded for the rest of the day. I made it through the day, however, and was off the next day.

I woke up and did some running around, picking up paperwork, and getting a little food. Then it happened again: I noticed my heart beating fast. This time, I began sweating badly too. I looked over to see if Anthony was looking, but he wasn't, so I kept quiet. When we made it back to his mom's house, I remembered that I'd forgotten to pick up something from Piggly Wiggly. When I walked into the store, I started shaking and sweating. I could hear my heart beating over the noises in the store. I took one step, and the ground felt like it was growing as I stepped. At this point, I was about to faint. I'd made a mistake and left my cellphone, but remembered that if I did happen to fall out, the assistant manager could call the ambulance and give them my info.

All of a sudden, I heard a young girl's voice say, "Hey, Meka. What are you doing?" I turned around, looking and feeling like everything was going in slow motion. It was my sister-in-law, Yandy, who also happens to be a nurse. God was really looking out for me. She looked at me and immediately knew that something wasn't right. I told her how I felt, so she called Anthony and told him what was happening. She checked my pulse and told Anthony and the friend she was with that she was going to drive the truck home. When we got home, the feeling stopped.

The same thing happened when I made it to work the next day. I cried and explained to the store manager that I didn't know what was wrong, but feared leaving because I needed my job. He told me to just bring a doctor's excuse, so I went to the emergency room at the hospital. After I explained my issues, the doctor said I was having an anxiety attack, which made my blood pressure rise significantly. It helped me understand why I couldn't be still and watch TV, was having such a hard time remembering things, needed medicine while in crowded environments, and felt so ill every time I parted from my family.

As a result of my nervous breakdown, I had to quit working at Piggly Wiggly. I had given up on everything but my kids. I was just sick of being sick and depressed. One particular night, I lay across our bed thinking of how I was always angry and arguing with Anthony, my sisters, and my mom about how I always fussed and cursed at the kids all the time. Anthony and my mom always struck a nerve when they brought up the fact that I whipped the kids for things I should've just talked to them about. Truthfully, I was just bitter and unhappy with myself and the reflection in the mirror.

One Friday night, I reached a point where I was ready to do whatever to take myself out. The devil took full control and my kids were completely out of mind. I had taken too many Lortab pain pills and some powerful prescription cough syrup that I was given when I had the flu a few weeks prior. I was high off of all these drugs I was using to relax my nerves which were buried in my misery, hurt, pain, and everything that wasn't godly. I walked in the living room where Anthony was watching television and cried, "Nard, I'm tired. I don't want to go on."

He said, "Tameka, what are you fucking talking about? We all need you. You have three beautiful kids that love and need you. I love and need you. Your mom, Billy, and your sisters all need you. God has you here for a reason. Come on, man. Don't ever say you're ready to take your life."

After a few days of resting and taking medication, I was back to myself. It took a few weeks, but I got back to the regular old Meka. The hard times were not over just yet though. Anthony and I were still pushing through and trusting in God for better days. I was about to turn 28 years old, and my mother and sister were planning a surprise party. They didn't want me to know anything, so I went along with the surprise. God knows I really needed some fun and laughter in my life.

On September 16th, 2011, they gave me the best birthday party of my life. Anthony stopped the music, asked for everyone's attention, and then dropped down on one knee and asked me to marry him. It took me about two minutes to say yes because I was crying just that hard. My ring was beautiful and fit perfectly. Later that night, he decorated the room with candles, rose petals, and lingerie. I cried again because this was a blessing from God. I woke up with Anthony next to me saying that he didn't want to wait long, so we set the wedding date in June.

Chapter 7

More Troubles

After a few months, my health did not improve much. For over a year, I'd been experiencing health issues which led to me taking more prescription medicine. After a year, we found that the medicine didn't help, so I sought further help. I agreed to have surgery, which was scheduled for February 6th at 6 AM. Anthony took me to the hospital in Tuscaloosa, where I prayed and asked God to hold my hand and take care of me.

Coming out of the surgery, I slept most of my overnight stay. The next morning, I remember the nurse waking me up to help me get dressed. I told her that I was hurting bad, so she told me the doctor would send me home with Lortab, Motrin, and one other prescription. When they finally discharged me, I went home and took a bite out of a potato that Anthony bought me, and it felt like my world was coming to an end. I thought it was gas, but it wasn't.

After a whole day of taking medication, I was still in pain. I called the doctor, and he asked if I had taken all the steps of relieving the pain provided when I left the hospital. If I'd taken the steps and I was still in pain, I should go back to the hospital. Once admitted, I had a fever of 103.5 and my blood pressure was extremely high, so they rushed me to the third floor to prep me for emergency surgery. When the first doctor performed my surgery, he didn't pay attention before finishing the surgery, causing a kink in my urethra which meant I was urinating out of my right kidney. As if that wasn't bad enough, the urine from my left kidney was backed up and mixing with my blood. The doctor who'd made the mistake openly stated to me, my mother, and Anthony that he wasn't aware of the kink because I was overweight. After hearing his excuse, I was pissed. The nurses knocked on the door to take me down for the second surgery, and the kidney specialist told me they were putting in a stint to help drain my left kidney.

In one week, I had back-to-back surgeries. After two of those surgeries, I woke up in recovery with broken promises and excessive pain and suffering. The fourth surgery sent me over the edge. Going into the surgery, I stressed about my left kidney. I was fed up with being locked in with no fresh air and no good results from the last couple of surgeries. I remember waking up on the operating table during the surgery, and it was freezing in the room. I could feel pulling and drilling on my body and began crying and screaming for help, but I didn't have much strength to scream very loudly. I noticed I was lying face down on a hard table, and as I screamed for help, I felt this deep stabbing pain in my left lower back. Before I saw any nurses or doctors, I heard some talking that sounded very far as if it was in a hallway. After that, I was out again.

When I woke up the second time, I was in my room. Struggling to hold my eyes open, I saw my fiancé, his mom, his sister and her three kids, my three kids, and my mom. Everyone's eyes were red, and Anthony was sitting with his head down looking at the floor. I looked down and saw the IV and some tubes in my hand, so I reached for the left side of my bed to sit up. I had a Nephrostomy tube in my left kidney which is why it felt as if they were pulling and jerking on my lower back; they were drilling a hole for the tube to thread it into my kidney.

Tears covered my chest, wet my gown, and helped stir the anger that overcame the fear that I would never be a normal 28-year-old woman again. As everybody in the room wiped their face, there was a knock on the door. The kidney specialist who performed the surgery walked in and told me they couldn't get the stint in because of the swelling from the first surgery. He also told me how important it was that I keep someone with me at all times considering I could no longer care for myself on my own. A nurse came in to explain to Anthony how to sanitize and hold the tube when he's caring for me, and they sent home healthcare personnel to my house weekly—sometimes twice a week depending on my blood pressure and temperature readings. This meant that Anthony could no longer work because he had to take care of me. After this mistake that the doctor made, I was thankful to have God on my side because it almost killed me.

Chapter 8

A Little Bit of Happiness

I applied for disability because I had no income and had to deal with constant back pain and other health problems. It hurt whenever it was cold outside, when I bent very low, or when I walked over a certain amount of time. The pain felt as though it cut my breathing short. I was in counseling for the tornado and the surgery, and I must admit it really helped me to relieve a good bit of anger. At one point, I felt like going in the doctor's office and hurting him because I wanted him to feel the pain I felt.

My application for disability was denied. Fortunately, Anthony went back to work in May of 2012. It took a while for me to find a job, but I finally did. However, I kept it a secret about wearing a tube and a bag because I didn't want anyone to have sympathy or to treat me any differently. One day, my tube started leaking on the job, so I had to rush to the bathroom. That day, I finally told my boss what was wrong with me and was able to get treated and return home.

God Had Other Plans

I decided then to take a break because it was almost time for my wedding.

I married Anthony on June 16th. I didn't know much about wedding planning, so I asked Angela and Tiffany, my grandmother's niece, to help me with things. Our wedding was at the McDonalds Hughes Community Center in Tuscaloosa, Alabama. I spent months preparing for our big day, and it was a blessing to get the tube and all my health issues taken care of before my bridal shower. My granny wanted to hire a wedding planner, Mrs. Prune. She supplied and cleaned up everything. The colors of our wedding were burnt orange, gold, off-white, and black. She started decorating that Thursday evening after the wedding practice, and it took her two and a half days to finish. She didn't want me to see the room because she wanted it to be a surprise. Mrs. Prune draped the walls with black and off-white fabric with lights underneath them. She covered the chairs with off-white fabric and the bow was burnt orange. The center pieces on the table looked like a tall champagne glasses with a lit floating candle.

The caterer for the wedding was my uncle, and my dad's cousin and my husband's cousin were both the photographers. The night before we married, all of the ladies and I went over to my mother's house for drinks and this wedding game that someone purchased. I really enjoyed each and every last one of my friends and family members. Angela treated me to getting my hair done and gave the kids a gift for the wedding. Ivina and my other friend bought my shoes as a gift, and my godmother purchased my wedding dress, jewelry and veil as a surprise.

Each time I received a gift, I cried because I knew it was God working in my favor. My family and friends really supported us. I had eight bridesmaids and groomsmen, five junior bridesmaids, and two flower girls. Our two daughters were the bride shadows. The two ring bearers ran around the room ringing a bell and screaming the bride is coming. My stepfather gave me away, and I cried my heart out. Once I walked in the room and saw all the people, I got nervous. However, as I approached my fiancé, I felt so blessed. The wedding was amazing!

The reception started and I thought Anthony would be scared to dance, but he wasn't; he was really excited. My mother and Anthony's daddy kicked it off after me and Anthony did our dance. My granny even came out on the dance floor. We then cut the cake and everybody ate. Once the kids left the building, we opened the bar. The reception ended around 11 PM, and my mother and friends loaded the gifts in the car. Anthony and I went home, celebrated together, and then went to bed. That day was one I will never forget. June 16th was one of the best days of my life.

Chapter 9

Another Loss

*I*t was the beginning of October 2012 that my granny started telling me that her stomach was hurting her. She said that one side was bigger than the other side. One morning she called and said that the ambulance was taking her to the hospital because she didn't feel well and couldn't breathe. I always got a little upset when my granny wanted to go to the hospital because she raised me, and she was and had always been a fighter. She spoke her mind even if she knew it would hurt someone. If it was going to help make them a better person in the future, then she was going to say it.

She admired Anthony and loved him with all her heart. She always bragged about how he stepped in and took care of my oldest daughter because her daddy wasn't in the picture. Every chance she got, she reminded me that I had a good man.

God Had Other Plans

After being in the hospital for two weeks, she was discharged. My mom picked her up, took her to the store for her medicine, and then took her home. They called my cellphone because my granny wanted me to come over to change her and make her bed. When I arrived at her apartment, she was sitting in her wheelchair. I tried to help her stand, but she had no strength. My mother and I had to get help, so we called my cousin. We tried everything, and by the time we got finished, she was sick and had to go back to the hospital. There, her health slowly deteriorated. She'd gotten to a point where she wouldn't even answer her room telephone, so I began worrying.

I went out to the medical center to check on her. When I entered the room, she was just lying there and looking at the wall. Each time I visited, it would be the same scenario. I would say, "Grandma, why you not answering the phone?" I tried my best not to show her I was angry though. She said, "Meka," with a frown on her face, "I just don't want to be bothered." On October 25th, she turned for the worse.

Earlier that week, my father had a stroke. All that weekend, he kept telling my mother that his head and stomach was hurting, but he would never listen when my mom told him to and go get checked. Monday morning, he woke up, got dressed, and went to work as normal. He's always talking, singing, or cracking jokes at my mom, but this morning, my mom noticed that he wasn't talking much.

On their way to his job, they stopped at the store for some gum. When my daddy went in to buy the gum, my mom said he came back out for some extra change. He was just saying, "ummmm" with his hand out as if he was asking for more change. He still didn't speak a word out of his mouth, so finally she dropped him off at work. He worked until about 11 AM when one of my dad's co-workers called my mom and said, "Faye, what's wrong with Billy today?" Momma asked her what happened, and she said that my dad hadn't said a word all day. When we talked to him, he would just kind of look away. She advised momma to talk him into getting checked out.

We got him checked out, and he had actually had a stroke. His mouth was twisted, his blood pressure was through the roof, and his blood sugar was also very high. God was there once again, and my dad pulled through. The doctors decided to keep him overnight to get him prepped for the medicine he would be taking daily. Tuesday morning, my mom and I went to see my daddy to make sure he was eating.

Afterwards, we went to the fifth floor to see my granny, but her room was empty. Immediately my heart dropped, and we looked at each other. After speaking with the nurse, we found out that she'd been moved to the Intensive Care Unit.

We had to visit my granny one at a time, so I wanted to go first. When I walked in, she was laying in the bed dozing off with her breakfast sitting on the table in front of her. She had a plateful that she hadn't even touched. I spoke softly, "Hey, Grandma. How you feeling? What all did the doctor say to you this morning?" She just stared at me. I stood beside her bed trying to get her to eat, but she only asked for the banana. She took two bites and went back to sleep. The nurse came in before I left and asked if we wanted to make a password. I said no and my granny grumbled, "Ummm hmmm" and frowned as if she meant what she said.

God, I puzzled my brain trying to figure out why she wanted me to set a password. After my mom headed in to see her, I sat there thinking, but couldn't wrap my head around it, so I just gave it to God. After my mom came out, we sat in the waiting area until around noon. I got ready to go in her room to tell my granny goodbye, and when I went in, I asked her if she was asleep.

"I'm about to go, so I can be close to the house when Nard call for me to pick him up from work," I said.

I was standing over by the window, glancing out at the cars when I heard her say, "I don't want you all to try and save me."

"What?" My heart began to sink, I couldn't feel my legs and my stomach was turning 150 miles per hour. "What are you talking about, Grandma?" I asked.

She said, "Meka, I'm tired. I just want to rest now." At this point, we're both crying, but I knew I had to pull it together. "You know where everything at, and I want to be buried in my dress that I wore to you and Nard's wedding." She told me to put the dress in the cleaners so it would be ready. My chest felt light. I heard her, but I didn't hear her.

I said, "Okay, Grandma. So you telling me that I need to go tell everybody that wants to see you that they need to come on now?"

She nodded her head real slow like she had no strength. She told me to tell our three children that she loves them and asked me to bring them as soon as they got out of school. She also told me to tell my mom, my cousin, and my godmother that she wanted them to help my mom and me with everything else. I told her that I loved her, kissed her, and left the room.

Now my mind was racing and my heart was beating fast because I had to face my mom, who was the only child that was left living since her baby brother passed away. He was the baby, and my mom was the oldest. I went and passed the news to my mother, who told me earlier that morning that she was stressed out because she was drained from running and trying to see about herself, my granny, and my daddy. She had just gotten out of the hospital two weeks before my daddy had his stroke, and now my granny talking about her days were about to end. She tried to make herself believe that my grandma was just talking out of her head since her blood was low and she was on so many medicines.

When I made it to my car, I cried again because I knew in my heart that Grandma was not just talking. I cleaned my face, called my godmother first, then I called my cousin's mother so she could pass the news on to my cousin. I didn't go into details with anyone, but I told everybody that it would be a good idea to go ahead and see her as soon as they could. I called and gave the nurse the password, told her what my granny said to me, and asked her if there was a letter in my granny's files stating that she did not want to be saved or put on a machine. She said no, so I asked her if it was okay to let my kids come back in the Intensive Care Unit to see their great-grandmother. She said, "Yes, just this one time." That happened on Tuesday.

I spent the next two days sitting in the room watching my granny while others came to visit. She laughed and talked with everyone. On Thursday I asked if that letter was on file, and the nurse said it was on file and signed. I asked if the doctor received my letter, and she told me that he had but she wasn't sure why he hadn't called yet. Later that night, most of the family gathered near her. We were all in the room standing over her bed looking at her because she would not wake up. After calling her for a while, she finally opened her eyes like she had only been ignoring us until she felt like talking. She bucked her eyes, slightly lifted her head, frowned at us, and asked, "What y'all looking at?" We all laughed then said, "You." She frowned and rolled her eyes. After that, she asked for our kids then went back to sleep. She was trying to fight it, but couldn't.

Friday, some of us were visiting granny in the hospital and she was not eating at all. She only slept, and the doctor said her stomach was beginning to swell worse than before. They let a specialist look at it, but he decided not to do the surgery. They said it wasn't anything they could really do at that point. When everyone else left, my cousin Alisha and I were sitting there watching the machine as my grandma slept. Every now and then, her heart rate would jump on a question mark. This was around 1:30 or 2 PM, then Alisha told Grandma that she'd be back later that night.

I had to leave too and was going to return after I picked up Nard and the kids, but I got tired. It was also past visiting hours, so I decided to go the next morning. Our house phone rang at 3:25 in the morning, and I instantly pushed the phone to my husband. My stomach was gone again. It was my mother. She told Anthony that we needed to hurry and get to the hospital. When I arrived at the hospital and stepped off of the elevator, I could hear some of my family members crying. I placed my hand up to the magnet to be let in, and when I walked through the doors, I immediately got weak. On my way to the room, it's like my hearing went away, my heart stopped, and my palms began to sweat. Shaking like a drug addict that needed a hit, I approached her bedside and just cried until there was a click in the back of my throat. Once I touched and kissed her, it was like, for a minute, everything was okay. I knew she was sick, but it was just the thought of knowing that I couldn't call her anymore that really hurt the most.

It was 5:05 and my mom, my cousin, and I were on our way to my granny's house to pick up all of the paperwork. We were all nervous about going to her house, but God gave us the strength to keep it together, gather everything we needed, and get out of there. In the car, Amy couldn't hold it anymore. She said that she was weak after thinking about how Grandma would no longer be there to talk to, see about, or even share the laughter. I think all three of our feelings had stepped in.

God Had Other Plans

My mom, my godmother, and I got together to look through all of the paperwork. My granny was a woman who didn't believe in waiting until the last minute to do things. She always took matters into her own hands. As we looked over her wishes, it was clear that she had planned and paid for her own funeral. She picked out the casket, the cemetery, the time, the church, and the pastor. She even had drawn an example of how the obituary should look. When everything was said and done, all we had to do was set the date and sign the paper at the funeral home. I always tell people that my granny definitely went out with a bang.

Chapter 10

A Fresh Start

Since my grandmother passed away, I'd been doing some serious thinking, looking back over my life and trying to make sense of everything that happened since the tornado. I started working again at the beginning of November 2012 at the hospital. I was working in the food service department, going to patients' rooms to take their orders for breakfast, lunch and dinner, but I only could work for two months, then I began to get sick again.

I came in contact with so many sick, healthy, but hurtful people who had so much pain and anger in them. I loved helping the patients, but the employees that I worked with, except about six of them, were so disrespectful to the patients in the hospital when it came to their privacy and health issues that I just could not deal with the job. After working there for about a month and a half, I put in my two weeks' notice.

Each morning, I started speaking positive things into my day. For months, I would get up, take my kids to school, and come back home and get on the computer. I stayed on it until it was time for me to pick up the kids. I would always cry when I was alone, thinking how hungry, yet helpless, I was for success. I would Google stars and foundations that helped struggling families achieve their dreams and goals. I would even call stars' managers to introduce myself and ask them to help me with things on my list, explaining that I just needed help getting started.

Time passed, and one afternoon in February, I was praying and telling God that today was the day I get a job before I returned back home. I was headed out to my mother's house and stopped to get a bite to eat. I was halfway past the entrance to a furniture store in town when I turned into the parking lot, got out the car, walked in the door, and spoke to the owner, Mr. Lilly. I asked him if he was doing any hiring. He said, "No, honey. What kind of experience do you have?"

I said, "Cashier, customer service, sales, stock, and a few others." He told me to go over and write some things about myself and my husband. When I returned to my car, I prayed. I knew God had already blessed me with that job, so I spoke it to my mother when I made it over her house. Later that day, the assistant manager called and asked me to come for an interview the next day. The following week I started working there and really enjoyed it. My co-workers were all like family, some of them were.

I started out as a clerk until they decided to put me on the sales floor with this wonderful man named Mr. Paul. Working with Mr. Paul was always interesting. He was very down to earth, and we would share our dreams and goals as small business owners. I began to notice that, at different times through my day, I would get this feeling, like a rush of power building up inside of me. As the feeling came over me, I would get over excited and want to run up to somebody and just tell them all that God had done for me.

Many times at work, I would go in the restroom, ball up in a knot, and cry. Then I would get up, clean up my face with water, and come out like nothing ever happened. My emotions were running wild. The power I felt made me feel like I could touch anything and make it come to life. I found that texting spiritual messages helped the feeling when it came over me. I kept this a secret for months until this lady came in the store and read me. It scared the heck out of me, but I stored the information that she gave me.

Chapter 11

God's Angel

Mrs. Tracie came in, went to the back counter, paid on her account, and then asked for help finding a matching rug for her living room. The assistant manager told my co-worker to help her to find what she was looking for.

Mrs. Tracie said, "I don't mean any harm, but I want that young lady to help me."

I smiled and headed towards her. "Hey, lady. How are you?"

She said, "Fine. I've been out all morning, witnessing for my father at the barber shop."

I said, "Okay. Well, what color is your living room?"

"Baby, what church you go to?" she asked.

"Elizabeth Baptist," I answered.

"You need to stop hiding what's in you and let it out."

"What are you talking about?" I asked, slowly backing away from her and looking around to see who was around us.

She said, "Let me show you what you do." She kneeled down in a knot, holding her stomach, moaning and groaning. At this point, I'm about to cry and I'm scared.

"God wants you to birth that baby," she said, pointing to my stomach. She smiled, then she quickly straightened her face and said, "Yeah, you pregnant, sister."

"What? Huh? My tubes are tied."

She laughed and said, "Not that kind of baby. God getting ready to use you, sister. You need to surround yourself with some good Christian people to let that baby in you out."

I shared the story with Nard about what Tracie told me. Tracie had invited me to church with her, but we never made it. I never forgot what she told me though. During a talk with my pastor once, he began to share with me how God had a calling on my life. I had no clue what that meant, but I remembered Tracie telling me that I needed to surround myself with more Christian people and to embrace what God wanted me to birth.

Mrs. Tracie began to position me and my husband in a circle with everyone we associated with around us. She explained to me that God was going to use us and described us as a powerhouse couple. She told me that my husband knew what God wanted, but that he was just surrounded by the wrong crowd. "But you, my sister, hold a key to so many people around you."

It was Saturday morning when I made it to work. I was feeling okay, but was really interested in a dream that I had the night before. While clocking in, I felt a little on the bright side, but I had to find out what that dream was about. Finally, the clerk came back to her desk. We talked before about sharing a dream, but this one really got me. Mrs. Angel is my amazing lady who helps me from time to time. She's very easy going and very mature in Christianity. After greeting her, I shared my dream with her, and she gave me some scriptures to read to try to help me understand the dream.

After reading the scriptures and thinking hard on some of the things Tracie had said to me, I decided to actually embrace whatever God was doing in my life. I began seeking help from God with my heart, mind, body, and soul. I prayed and asked God to deliver me from drinking, the cursing, grudges, anger, and so much extra pain from hurt in my past. I began to let God take full control of me. It got to the point where my stomach would hurt every time I took a drink, so I didn't even want liquor or beer. People who I dealt with in the past, who I knew didn't give two cents about me, I finally counted out. I could no longer sit in a room where people were gossiping about another human being. I was done and hungry for nothing and no one but God and His word.

Chapter 12

God Has Other Plans

While working at the furniture store, my mother and my father were often sick. My mother was having back-to-back surgeries, or so it seemed. She would pick up our kids when I was working or whenever Anthony had to work. I wanted to take that pressure off of my mother and be by her side whenever she and my daddy got sick, so I decided to step out on faith and get a business license. I made flyers to pass around the community, introducing my cleaning business, One Time Cleaning, to the public until I got business cards.

I prayed and talked to God before I let my job go. That following morning I went to work and thought about it. When I got another phone call stating that my mother had to have surgery the next day, I told God that I was going to let his will be done. I decided during my break that I had to take care of my children and be there for my mother and father like they were there for me when I was sick.

God Had Other Plans

When I quit my job, Anthony was still working. He told me to just take care of home and the kids and that he would handle the rest. I knew it was God's will for me to quit my job because my mother has not been sick like that again since I let it go. My daddy had another stroke, and this time I was able to be there with him every morning, even if it was just to sit there. God worked it out, and he started doing a whole lot better.

In the past, I was denied disability, but I appealed my case. I couldn't get a lawyer to take my case because they all felt I didn't have one. My cleaning service didn't have much business, but I was still glad that I could work my own schedule and be able to take and pick my children up from school every day. I made it to every program and honor assembly like a mother should. I did end up looking for a part-time job, but after two interviews and not hearing from either of them after several months, I took it as a sign to spend that time with God. To this day, God is showing me a new gift. At night I don't even sleep because I'm up with the Holy Ghost. If I do sleep, He's showing me things in my dreams for others.

The day before my court date, I dropped the kids off at school and Anthony at work. I used my alone time to pray, read my bible, and witness to serve as a servant of the Lord on Facebook and everywhere else I went. My cellphone rang with a message from a young lady I knew who is also very mature in the Christian world. She'd sent me a song called "Breaking Every Chain" by Tasha Cobbs. I started listening to the song and tears began rolling down my face. I stopped the song and called her.

"Good morning! How you doing?" she asked.

"Thank you, Trenda. I needed that," I said.

She said, "You were on my mind all night. I tried to send you a message on Facebook, but I couldn't," she continued, "God wants you to know that He got this and He just want you to trust in Him."

I said, "Yes ma'am, thanks for the word."

She instructed me to close my eyes and listen to that song, so I went to my worship room in our house and did just that. About four hours later that day, the lady from Lowe's Home Improvement called and asked me to be at an interview that Friday morning at 11 AM. The next day was my court day for the disability case. I pulled up about fifteen minutes early and prayed until it was time to go in.

I told God, "Okay, I'm putting on my armor and we're going in." The devil tried to fool me into thinking that I was going to faint and even tried to make me think I was having an anxiety attack. Every time someone and their lawyer came in, he tried to steal my trust in my God. *Oh no, not the God I serve*. The lady came to the door and called my name, and God held my hand every step of the way. When God got done working in the midst of it all, it was signed, sealed, and delivered. I won my case.

God is renewing, replacing, rewarding and revealing in my life. He has placed so many amazing women in my life. I'm talking about positive women with real love who are ready to help me grow into my destiny. As I speak, God is still delivering me from so many things and people. While doing so, He has given me some gifts to witness for Him. I now understand that I was going through everything in order to be placed in the position that God wanted me in. Now my job title is Servant for God, and my pay is happiness, joy, love, and peace. My benefits are gifts from God that help others. As for now, look out for what is coming next as

God continues to use me because this is only the beginning of my story!

To be continued......

About Tameka Hope

TAMEKA HOPE is a motivational speaker, author and the CEO of Faithful Printing and Apparel. She has a passion of helping others turn their dreams into accomplished goals.

Having nearly lost everything in Tuscaloosa's 2011 EF4 tornado, she has a heart to bless the homeless and the abused, giving them the support and encouragement to rebuild on a foundation of self-love and purpose.

Devoted to the word of God, Tameka's mission is to lead the lost to Christ and help the determined find their destiny to reach for the stars. "I want to birth a worldwide movement for strong, powerful sisters who love God and don't mind speaking to and uplifting the next sister or brother."

In addition to ministering God's word and designing clothes, Tameka also enjoys traveling the world and dreams of one day becoming a playwright and screenwriter. Until then, she comfortably resides in her hometown of Tuscaloosa, Alabama with her husband, Anthony, two daughters, Ta'Mya and Zahria, and son, Anthony Jr.

TO LEARN MORE ABOUT TAMEKA, VISIT:

www.About.Me/TamekaHope

  tameka.hope.5

www.ingramcontent.com/pod-product-compliance
Lightning Source LLC
Chambersburg PA
CBHW052115070526
44584CB00017B/2494